Riddle Romp

by
Giulio Maestro

CLARION BOOKS
TICKNOR & FIELDS: A HOUGHTON MIFFLIN COMPANY
NEW YORK

Clarion Books
Ticknor & Fields, a Houghton Mifflin Company

Library of Congress Cataloging in Publication Data
Maestro, Giulio.
Riddle romp.
Summary: A collection of original riddles designed to
increase vocabulary.
1. Riddles, Juvenile. [1. Riddles. 2. Vocabulary]
I. Title.
PN6371.5.M29 1983 818'.5402 83-2067
ISBN 0-89919-180-0
Paperback ISBN 0-89919-207-6

V 10 9 8 7 6 5 4 3 2 1

How does a bee clean up spilled pollen?

With a bloom and dustpan.

When does a rocket get hungry?

When it's almost launch time.

Why didn't the fork take a stab at the meatballs?

It was pointless.

How can you tell when holly berries are happy?

They're wreathed in smiles.

How did the banana eat her ice cream?

Lickety split.

Why don't pine trees mind being teased?

They're used to being needled.

What kind of boat always gives you
a sinking feeling?

A failboat.

What drink do you make with sour fruit?

Gripe juice.

What vegetable do you eat before summer squash?

Spring beans.

Why can't you trust a shark?

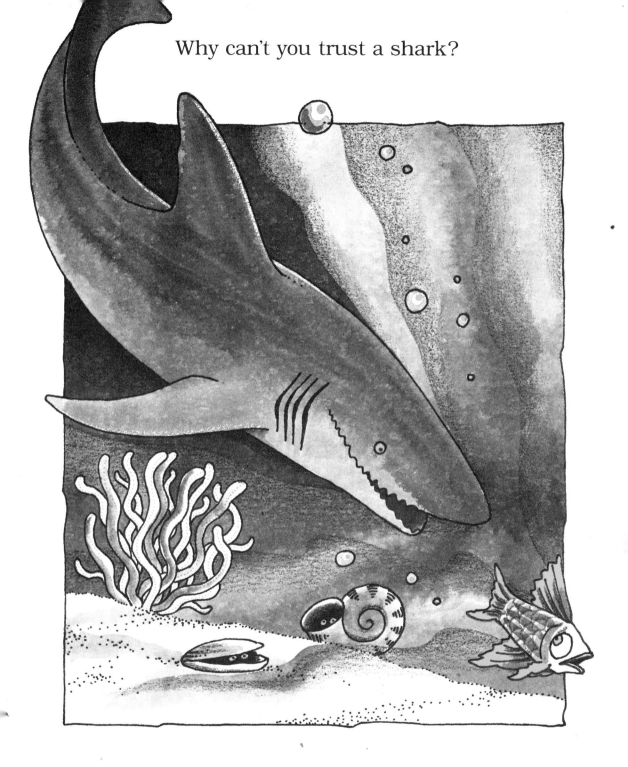

There's something fishy about him.

How does ketchup feel when it's
near a hamburger?

It relishes every moment.

What is the opposite of an open door
with no clothes on?

A clothed door.

Why can't cacti get along with
each other?

They have abrasive personalities.

How did the knife flatter the roll?

She buttered him up.

What's a sweet, red fruit with an
honest face?

A candid apple.

When does a baseball player wear armor?

During a knight game.

Who goes to great lengths to steal overshoes?

A rubber bandit.

What do you call a cake decorated with diamonds?

A very rich dessert.

Who is a smoothie outside, and a spicy character inside?

A deviled egg.

Why did the fussy porcupine pick
a bed of nails?

It had many strong points.

Why do fish make a good swim team?

They pool their talents.

What's the best way to clear your mind?

With a brainwashing.

Why did the captain dock his ship
near a barber shop?

He needed a crew cut.

What did the artist use to color
her valentine cards?

A paint blush.

What does a frog do when he has a flat?

He calls for a toad truck.

How do you know when food doesn't want
to be eaten?

When it's revolting.

Why was the construction worker
attached to his job?

He was riveted to the spot.

Why is a rock always in shock?

Because it's petrified.

Why didn't the police officer believe the corn cob's story?

There wasn't a kernel of truth in it.

When are ocean waves sad?

When they're crestfallen.

Why is a crab like a plumber's wrench?

He's good in a pinch.

How did the thief make a pig
of himself?

He was a hamburglar.

How did the trombonist find a place
in the marching band?

He horned in.

How can you tell when an ice cube
is nervous?

It breaks out in a cold sweat.

Why is it easy to fool a sheep?

You can always pull the wool over her eyes.

Why couldn't the mechanic tear himself
away from his cars?

He was caught in their clutches.

What change in the weather has a sharp bite?

A cold snap.

Why do sponges do a good job?

They become absorbed in their work.

What water sport does a racehorse like?

Steed-boating.

What candies do hummingbirds eat?

Humdrops.

What starts out battered and ends up flattened?

A pancake.

What stories do baby oranges like?

Tales of Mother Juice.

What do Christmas carolers eat on the run?

Hasty pudding.

Why are high-wire artists always nervous?

They're so high-strung.

Why did the bookworm have an upset stomach?

He couldn't digest all the facts.

How does a band serve up tasteful tunes?

With drum rolls.

What buzzed around King Arthur's head?

The Gnats of the Round Table.

Why did the musician cry after losing
his drum?

He missed the beat.

Why does a traveling singer take an
extra suitcase?

So she can carry a tune.

How was the baked potato covered with praise?

The butter gave it pats on the back.

What can you do when you're attacked by mosquitoes?

Call in the SWAT team.

Why was the headless horseman always
losing his way?

He was absent-minded.

Why does a porcupine always win an argument?

She knows how to get her points across.

What kind of beans glow at night?

Moon beans.

Why are baby ghosts so cute?

Because they're not yet fully groan.

What do you call two rabbits with one
meatball between them?

Hamburger bunnies.

Why are eggs always so serious?

They don't dare crack a smile.

Where do bees stay when they're just married?

In the honeymoon suite.

Who do big ships fear will push
them around?

Thug boats.

What do you bake for a police officer
on her birthday?

A copcake.

How did the little girl like her
balloon ride?

She found it an uplifting experience!